HOW TO WIN!

A GUIDE TO SUSTAINABLE SUCCESS WORKBOOK

DR. JOSPEH D. REID, CPA

LAEL PUBLISHING

HOW TO WIN!
A Guide to Sustainable Success Workbook
by Dr. Joseph D. Reid, CPA
Published by Lael Publishing, LLC
Winston-Salem, North Carolina
www.LaelAgency.com

No part of this book may be used or reproduced in any form, stored in a retrieval system, or transmitted in any form by any means, electronic, photocopy, mechanical, recording or otherwise without written permission from the author. The only exception is for critical articles or reviews, in which brief excerpts may be used.

ISBN 978-1-7325344-1-4
Copyright © 2018 by Dr. Joseph D. Reid, CPA
All Rights Reserved

First Edition

Printed in the United States of America.

TABLE OF CONTENTS

Section 1
Finding Your Individual Path to Success..7

Section 2
Leadership: Empowerment for Sustainable Success................15

Section 3
The Tools of Sustainable Success..19

Section 4
Cultivating a Success Mindset..23

Section 5
Prospect: 10 Components..33

Section 6
Plan: 10 Components..47

Section 7
Execute: 10 Components..63

Section 8
Bringing it all Together..77

SECTION 1

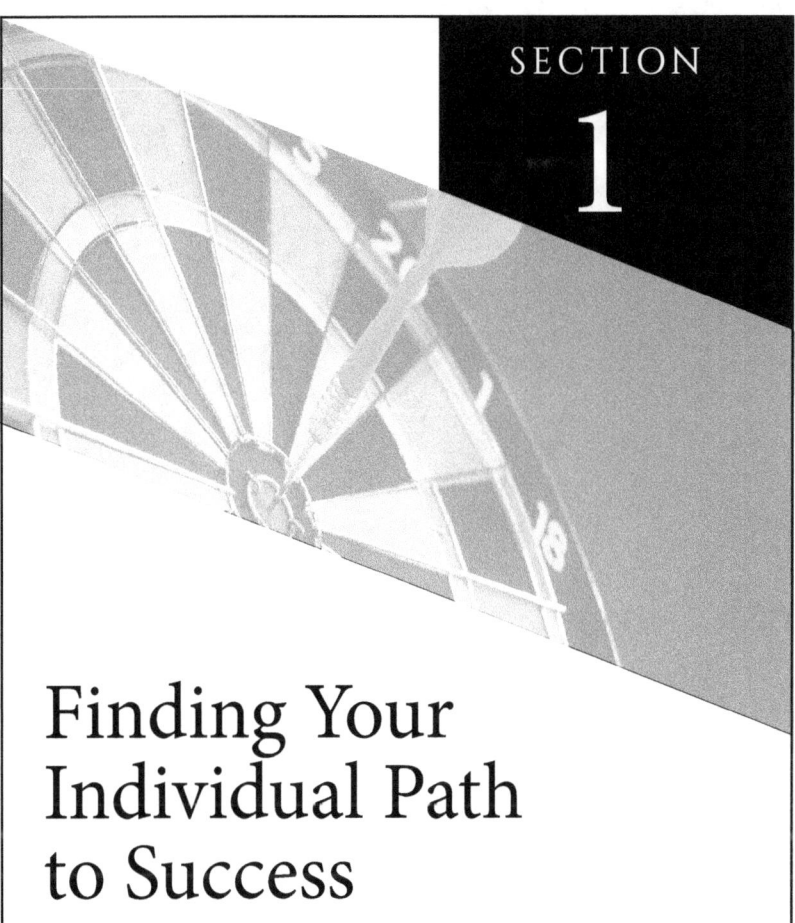

Finding Your Individual Path to Success

Finding Your Individual Path to Success

How do you define success in your career and work life?

_____

_____

_____

_____

_____

Is it about a certain income level?

_____

Is it about promotions received, deals brokered, or sales made?

_____

Is it about knowing that you've made a difference in the world through your work and by having a genuine commitment to better those whose lives you impact?

_____

_____

_____

Success is defined by both internal and professional elements.

What are the many paths you can take to achieve the success you desire?

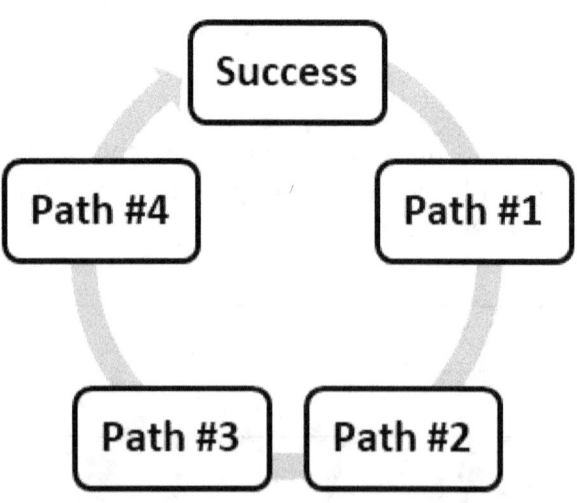

Finding Your Individual Path to Success

Path #1:

_____

_____

Path #2:

_____

_____

Path #3:

_____

_____

Path #4:

_____

_____

HOW TO WIN! A Guide to Sustainable Success Workbook

Use the space below to list out the common elements involved in the achievement of success, in your experience.

-
-
-
-
-
-
-
-

"Harnessing the power of economic collectivism helps to create sustainable success in business projects and the evolution of a career."

Finding Your Individual Path to Success

Qualities of being committed to your goal:

What knowledge and education are required to achieve your goal?

_____

_____

What are your strengths and weaknesses relative to achieving your goal?

_____

_____

What does it mean to manage adversity and mitigate risk relative to your goals?

_____

_____

SECTION 2

Leadership: Empowerment for Sustainable Success

Leadership: Empowerment for Sustainable Success

One of the most defining characteristics of a successful career trajectory is the development of leadership abilities.

In the space below, list out the abilities and characteristics that one would need to be a leader or that you have seen in a good leader:

While the skills of leadership may manifest by rising to higher levels of management within an organization or taking on more prominent roles in the business world, it can also take the form of your emergence as a thought leader in your chosen field.

The characteristics of effective leadership can be cultivated through:

- deliberate intention
- focus
- seeking mentorship

Write a list of potential mentors:

Name	Contact Info

SECTION

3

The Tools of
Sustainable
Success

The Tools of Sustainable Success

Empowerment comes through seeking resources of motivational self-help geared toward enhanced personal development.

What are some resources you currently need to help you achieve your goals?

_____

_____

_____

_____

_____

_____

_____

_____

_____

"You CAN create the successful work life and career path you've always dreamed of, and it begins with the desire to do so. If you've gotten this far, you clearly have that."

SECTION

4

Cultivating a Success Mindset

Cultivating a Success Mindset

There is a mindset that creates and defines success, and it is foundational to any future successes. Instead of being a mystical or elusive "holy grail," success is comprised of simple yet effective concepts and tools. If we could distill the formula for a winning strategy of sustainable success down to its most basic components, they would include the following three phases:

       1. Prospect
       2. Plan
       3. Execute

1. Prospect

The Prospect Phase is a time to look for possibilities and thoroughly vet them to choose the ideas that are the most fertile and aligned with your current objectives. Perhaps you already have an idea for your next goal in raw form? However, prospecting also involves researching the viability of each new idea and assessing the likelihood of its success.

What is one idea that you would like to consider as a potential goal?

_____

Is there a market for that particular product, service, or business idea?

_____

Is there a career role within your reach that fits your deepest and most authentic hopes and expectations?

_____

If you determine that an idea is simply not viable during this phase, go back to the drawing board and find one that is.

Use the space below to do any revamping to your idea that you might need.

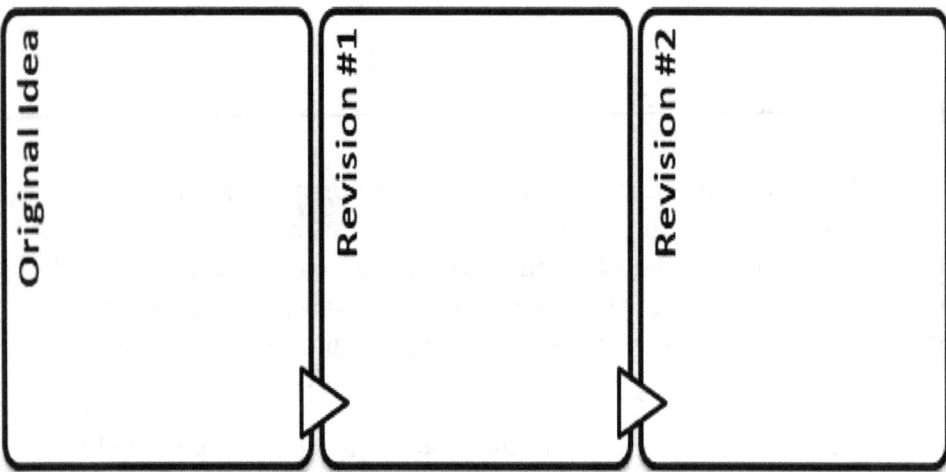

Be transparent and honest enough to walk away from ideas that simply are not realistic or sustainable.

2. Plan

Once the viability of a business goal or career plan has been established, Planning is the essential next phase. A business plan outlines the steps needed to manifest entrepreneurial goals.

Your plan will likely include elements related to financing your idea such as buying supplies, hiring required personnel, identifying vendors and finding the right location. It needs to include specific action steps towards your goal. Use the space below to help you brainstorm those ideas.

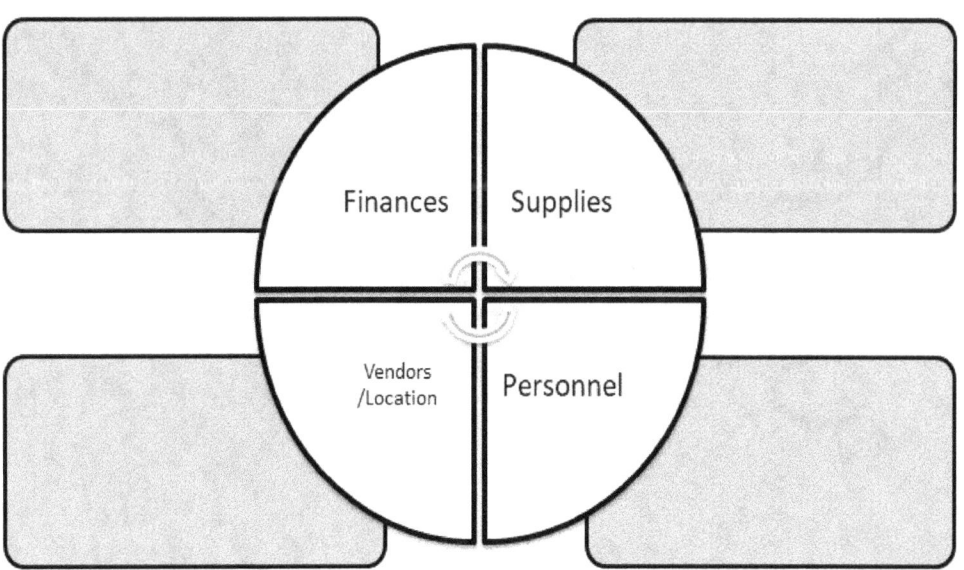

Brainstorm how you can move from your current role to your desired new position:

Use the space below to list networking opportunities, additional training you may need, and research on potential companies and employers.

Networking	Additional training	Potential companies and employers

"While you certainly shouldn't dwell excessively on negative potentials, being aware of the most likely obstacles and challenges before they happen is part of a sustainable winning strategy."

3. Execute

Once your goals and ideas are solidified into a well-researched plan with specific action steps, it's time to take action. The Execution Phase is the time for bringing your vision to life, and the time frame for this phase of goal achievement is the most variable. The Execution phase of goal achievement requires drawing from the very best of your personal qualities and effectively managing your weak areas.

Take a moment and list your strengths and weaknesses.

Strengths	Weaknesses
☐	☐
☐	☐
☐	☐
☐	☐

"Areas where you don't excel or do not feel connected to should be outsourced to people proficient in the skills required to effectively complete them."

Within each of the three phases, there are 10 components to success:

- Commitment and Faithfulness
- Education
- Self-Sufficiency
- Transparency
- Self-Awareness
- Leverage
- Patience
- Infrastructure
- Adversity
- Risk Mitigation

These components are not defined or applied the same within each phase. Mastery and proper implementation of these 10 components within the phases of Prospecting, Planning and Execution, helps to provide both knowledge of self and a template for sustainable success.

SECTION

5

Prospect: 10 Components

Prospect: Commitment and Faithfulness

Is your goal an idea that you are likely to stay faithful to, or are your values and perceptions around it subject to change?

_____

_____

_____

How faithful and steadfast can you be to this goal?

_____

_____

_____

Is this something you feel passionate about? _____

For more insights during the crucial goal selection phase, ask yourself: "Why do I want to pursue this goal?"

_____

_____

_____

Prospect: Education

Educating yourself about market conditions, competitors and what your goal really requires is paramount to sound decision-making and proceeding effectively.

Use the space below to list out additional training, classes, or education you may need to increase your chances of being chosen for a new position or that will help take your business/goals to the next level.

Class/Training/ Education	Amount of time to complete	Cost/Benefit

Prospect: Self-Sufficiency

The cultivation of a goal that is as self-sustaining as possible is another key to success.

What drives you?

_____

_____

What aspects of your business life or career are so inspiring that they do not feel like work?

_____

_____

_____

_____

The answers to these questions should inform your prospecting and goal-setting choices. Making choices using these guidelines will greatly enhance your ability to stay with and see your goals through to fruition.

How self-sufficient are you personally?

_____

_____

_____

_____

Prospect: Transparency

How honest can you be with yourself? The time for total transparency from an internal perspective is now, during the crucial Prospect Phase.

Make an honest assessment of your strengths and weaknesses and how they might apply to each goal.

Strengths:
How can you improve them? How will they benefit your goals?

-
-
-
-

Weaknesses:
How can you improve them? If unfixed, how can they hurt your goals?

-
-
-
-

What are your deepest reasons and motivations for wanting to pursue them?

_____
_____
_____
_____
_____
_____
_____

Prospect: Self-Awareness

So much about goal setting and being successful has its roots in self-awareness. If you choose goals that don't sync up with both your strengths and your weaknesses, you are far less likely to succeed and achieve them.

Use the space below as a self-awareness check. Add additional questions to ask yourself.

Self-Awareness Check	Yes	No
Do you have the funding?		
Will this be profitable?		
Is there a market for your idea?		

A thorough Prospect Phase is essential to success, and self-awareness is the key to making the right decisions during this foundational step.

Prospect: Leverage

Leverage refers to the resources you currently have at your disposal to make pursuing and achieving your goals easier.

What goals can be most easily leveraged in your current situation?

_____

_____

_____

"Think creatively and be open to how elements of your current situation could lay the groundwork for greater heights of success going forward."

Prospect: Patience

Patience is an extremely important virtue, and everyone can benefit from having a healthy measure of it. However, patience is of particular value to those who wish to continually build on past successes and ascend to greater heights of personal achievement.

Take a moment and really think about this question. What things can cause you to lose patience? How will these things effect your future?

_____

_____

_____

Think of a time when someone was impatient with you while you were doing your best. How did it feel?

_____

_____

"Cultivate patience and make the most of your time as you wait for outcomes to come to fruition in perfect time."

Prospect: Infrastructure

As you engage in the Prospect Phase and work with the raw energies of brand new ideas, you should also keep an eye toward the structure or infrastructure that will be required to bring a goal or idea to fruition.

If it is a product or service idea, what resources, vendors, materials and framework will be required to help make it a reality?

_____
_____
_____
_____
_____

"Your infrastructure is the backbone and skeletal system of your idea."

What form will the framework of your idea take?

_____
_____
_____
_____
_____

Prospect: Adversity

While you don't want to dwell on or plan for negative occurrences, it is always wise to consider how adversity might arise on your chosen path.

Outline potential adversities on the diagram below.

What personal qualities do you have that will help you to navigate and get through adversity?

_____
_____
_____

What characteristics could be developed or brought out more?

_____
_____
_____
_____
_____
_____

"Anticipating possible challenges and adversities on the path to your goal can assist you in accessing the qualities necessary for overcoming them."

Prospect: Risk Mitigation

This component of the Prospect Phase goes hand in hand with mapping out adversities. Once you have delineated the potential challenges that could factor into a business idea or career goal, consider how the risks might be mitigated.

Potential Adversity	How will it be mitigated?

SECTION

6

Plan:
10 Components

Plan: Commitment and Faithfulness

The considerations of commitment and faithfulness are very important when creating and executing a plan. In the plan creation phase, crafting components that are easy to follow, implement, and stick to increases the odds for success.

Is your plan constructed in such a way that its parts are easy to follow and progress easily determined?

_____

_____

_____

_____

How committed and faithful can you be to the plan?

_____

_____

_____

_____

You should ask yourself this often as you devise, create and refine it. A plan is only as successful as your commitment to it and ability to follow it.

Use the space below to create and refine your plan.

Original Plan	Revised Plan

Plan: Education

When covering the steps required to achieve your goal and formulate your plan, additional research or training may be needed to do all phases full justice. Carefully consider the educational aspects of a business or career plan. If you are a serial entrepreneur, you likely have a core set of skills from which you can draw when forming new businesses.

Use the diagram below to show what additional education/ training you will need, as well as skills and research to continue you build on your goals.

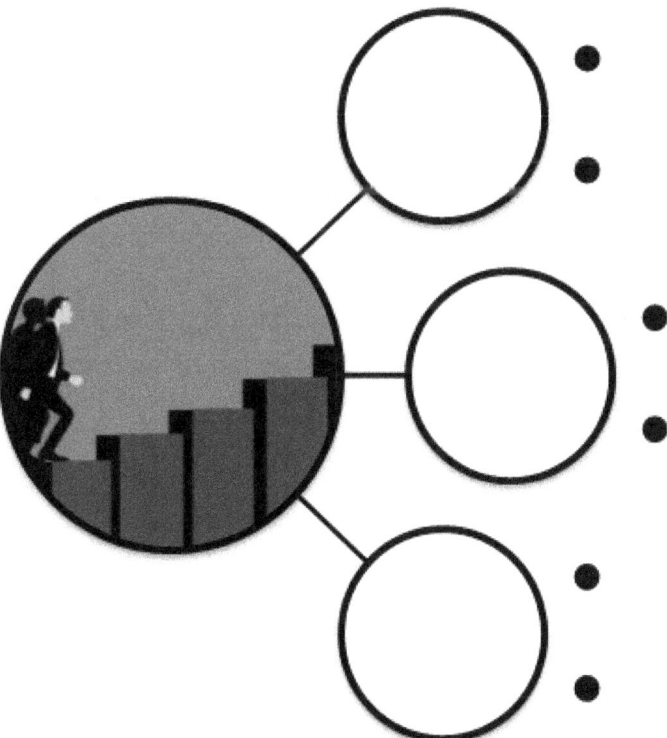

Plan: Self-Sufficiency

Your degree of self-sufficiency should also factor into the nature and structure of the plan you create. The more self-sufficient you are, the smoother any plan will go. However, lower amounts of self-sufficiency can be offset by outsourcing key portions of a plan to qualified parties.

> ➢ Strive to apply self-sufficiency to your business goal and plan.

How self-sustaining are your methods and outcomes?

_____

_____

"There is great value in striving for these qualities, as their presence will make life easier in all phases of goal setting and achievement."

Plan: Transparency

Be transparent with yourself and relevant parties as you

Plan: 10 Components

formulate your plan.

How realistic is your plan and your role in it?

_____

_____

_____

_____

What portions of your plan can be outsourced?

_____

_____

_____

In light of your current skills and personal qualities, is your career goal realistic? If not, is there a more realistic goal that will take you in the direction of your ultimate career goals?

_____

_____

_____

_____

How will the people in your professional and personal life respond and factor into these goals?

_____
_____
_____
_____
_____
_____
_____
_____
_____
_____

"Be transparent with all other parties involved in your plan and require the same from them. Transparency and honesty are keys to effective communication, so striving for this during your plan formulation phase increases your odds of success."

Plan: Self-Awareness

A deep awareness of who you are, including your strengths and weaknesses, is essential when crafting a plan of action to take your goals from vision to reality.

Go back to the beginning stages of your plan and revamp those strengths and weaknesses. Add any additional questions.

Self-Awareness Check	Yes	No
Do you need to outsource work to others?		
Have you revised any parts of the plan?		
Are there items that need to be removed?		

"If you find your goal requires a plan with a majority of elements that aren't a fit for you, you may want to reconsider if that goal is really right for you."

HOW TO WIN! A Guide to Sustainable Success Workbook

Plan: Leverage

An awareness of existing opportunities that you can leverage within future goals and endeavors is particularly important in the planning phase of goal setting. In the entrepreneurial space, leverage your existing knowledge base to fuel the creation of new businesses.

How can supply chains, vendors, and related resources be accessed and used in new projects?

_____
_____
_____
_____
_____
_____
_____
_____
_____

"Look for ways to avoid reinventing the wheel as you create your plan for new projects."

Plan: Patience

All plans take time to implement and come to fruition. Have patience with yourself as you craft, refine, and add the required details to your plan.

Which areas of your plan will require the most patience?	What support and additional resources will you need?

"Patience is especially important when setting and pursuing personal career goals. Strive to continually cultivate the quality of patience and be aware of how it may apply in current and future scenarios during the plan creation phase."

Plan: Infrastructure

An awareness of the required structuring and infrastructure required to bring it to fruition should factor into the plan creation process.

If it is a product or service idea, what resources, vendors, materials and framework will be required to help make it a reality?

_____

_____

_____

_____

_____

As you create your plan, what framework will your success take?

_____

_____

_____

_____

Plan: 10 Components

Plan: Adversity

Thinking about what could go wrong isn't negative as long as you can keep an eye toward positive resolutions to every possible delay or setback.

As you craft your plan, think about what obstacles and challenges might come up as you pursue it. Make a comprehensive list and consider the best possible and most effective solutions ahead of time.

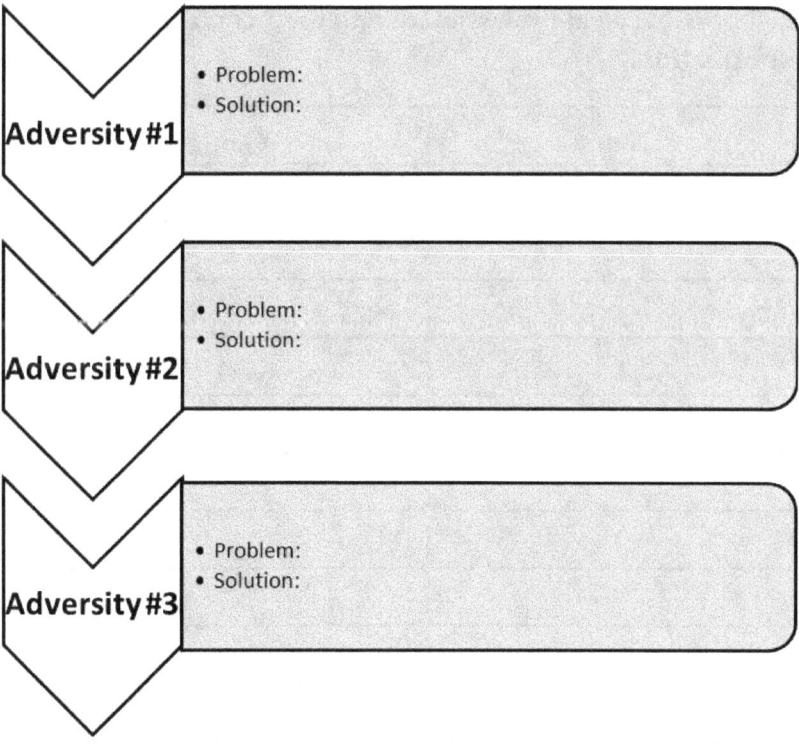

Plan: Risk Mitigation

Risk management in the planning phase goes hand in hand with mapping out possible adversities.

If required, consult with a legal professional or someone experienced in your areas of concern.

List possible legal professionals and their contact information.

Name	Contact

Plan: 10 Components

How can the following items help with risk mitigation?

Insurance	
Back-up plans	
Added security	
Other fail safes	

"Learn to see that it isn't a matter of "either-or," but instead a smart and realistic attitude regarding what could go wrong as you pursue your goals."

SECTION 7

Execute: 10 Components

Execute: Commitment and Faithfulness

The qualities of commitment and faithfulness are crucial to the Execution Phase. They will determine if you see your goal through as well as the quality and efficiency of your actions. By the time you've entered the Execution Phase of your project, your commitment and resolve will have been well established. However, staying committed to your plan and faithful to your goals will be tested the most stringently during this phase.

Take a moment and remind yourself of your "why." What is your why? What motivates you?

_____

_____

_____

_____

_____

Stay closely connected to the "why" of career goals and objectives as well. You are likely hoping to both assist customers and be a part of a team that's aligned with a common goal. You may also wish to improve the lives of your family members and others that will benefit from your promotion. Let these factors motivate you to stay faithful and committed to the goal you've set forth and the plan you have crafted to help bring it into reality.

Execute: Education

Education and training required for meeting and achieving your goal will likely already have taken place in the Prospect and Planning phases. However, be open and ready to undertake additional education and training as the execution of your plan takes place.

Seek out mentors and resources every step of the way, and especially during the Planning and Execution phases.

List out your mentors and resources.

Mentors	Resources

Execute: Self-Sufficiency

Self-sufficiency is extremely important to success and goal realization in the Execution Phase. Having the discipline to follow your plan and see every element through to its optimal conclusion is essential to success. By this phase you will have already considered how your level of self-sufficiency might affect the Planning and Execution phases of your goal.

Now is the time to tap into your ability to follow a plan and stay aligned with the vision that inspired your goal in the first place. Fueled by a deep personal alignment with your goal as a calling, you will already be strengthened and emboldened to push past your previous limits.

Remind yourself of your "why" when things are not moving smoothly. Re-write your why below.

_____

_____

_____

"Tap into your own reserves of self-will to help see your efforts through to a winning conclusion."

Execute: Transparency

In the Execution Phase of any goal, it is important to make note of where you are energized and on target and where you might be falling short. Inner honesty and transparency is an important key to staying on track with your plan and ultimately the manifestation of your goals.

Take time to do a transparency check. Ask yourself the following questions.

Have you been completely honest with yourself? Business partners, employees, etc.?

_____

Have you followed all the steps of your plan?

Have you revised your plan to align with any adversities and challenges you have encountered along the way?

"Begin these relationships on the right foot and stay committed to transparency and honesty throughout your connection with them. It is key to successful relationships and ultimately the viability and impact of your project."

Execute: Self-Awareness

By this stage of the game, you should be quite self-aware. In the Prospect Phase, you will have looked at how your personality would mesh with your goals and ideas for your work life and career path. In the Planning Phase, you tailored your action steps in a way that was aligned with who you are and your strengths and weaknesses.

Dig deep during these times to find the skills and qualities within you that you know can pull you through. In the space below, discuss the characteristics that were revealed in the pursuit of your goal and how you can apply them going forward. Provide specific examples.

_____
_____
_____
_____

"In pursuing and achieving every new goal, your sense of self-awareness will broaden and deepen, paving the way for even greater levels of success going forward."

Execute: Leverage

The resources you identified and leveraged during the Prospecting and Planning phases will come into focus during the Execution Phase. Now, it will be time to tap into these resources in the most optimal ways possible. The goal is to help streamline the implementation process and connect with the most efficient and effective pathways to success.

Now is the time to implement the plans you set forth in the last phase.

Are you taking advantage of all of the resources you currently have at your disposal to make manifestation of your goals as easy and effortless as possible?

_____

_____

When pursuing a promotion or other opportunity within an existing company or chosen sector, take advantage of helpful resources such as management advice, supportive colleagues and in-house training opportunities. List those resources below:

_____

_____

_____

_____

List any additional opportunities for leverage to help you achieve success.

_____

_____

> *"Remember that just about anything can be a resource that functions as leverage to help you to achieve your goals."*

Execute: Patience

Patience during the Execution phase will largely mirror what you have mapped out and anticipated during the Planning phase. However, patience will be critical if delays or unexpected obstacles arise as you are executing your plan.

The cultivation of patience can be supported by a spiritual practice or by drawing from relevant life experiences. List ways below that will help improve your patience.

_____

_____

_____

_____

Describe a time when someone was impatient with you and how that made you feel.

_____

_____

_____

_____

It is a virtue to be able to be patient in such situations. You'll be less stressed out in the pursuit of your goals and better able to continue on your path toward their realization.

Execute: Infrastructure

By the Execution Phase of goal achievement, the required infrastructure will have already been considered. As you execute your plan, this structure will begin to take shape and either embody your vision or require changes. As this occurs, be aware of any additions or refinements that might enhance the unfolding of your plan in service to your goal. Add to and refine what you are creating to support your new project or goal.

Engage the framework for success that you brainstormed in the Planning Phase. Refine the components of your infrastructure as required or as conditions change. Stay aligned with all of the elements of your infrastructure both literal and energetic in terms of support, and you'll pave the way to achievement and success. Make revisions below.

_____

_____

_____

_____

_____

_____

Execute: Adversity

How you handle adversity within the Execution Phase of your business or personal career plan will determine the ease with which your goal can be accomplished. The Execution Phase is the time when you could potentially face the most adversity.

This is the time when your inner work and awareness related to patience, self-sufficiency, and other positive qualities can be a source of strength that helps you power through adversities of all kinds.

In the space below take another look at any potential adversities and write how it may affect your execution phase.

_____

_____

_____

_____

_____

_____

_____

_____

"Choose to see the "gift" or learning experience in every adversity."

Execute: Risk Mitigation

Again, once you've delineated the potential challenges to your business ideas or career goals in the Prospect and Plan phases, you will have taken the necessary steps to mitigate most foreseeable and likely risks. Risk mitigation in this phase refers to your ability to deflect any negativity or energies that are contrary to your objective.

Again, the goal is avoiding obstacles and major challenges altogether if possible, but if they do arise, you should already have sound, thoughtful responses in place to mitigate risk and its potential impact.

HOW TO WIN! A Guide to Sustainable Success Workbook

Use the space below to detail positive affirmations that can be used to assist you in maintaining the appropriate perception

_____
_____
_____
_____
_____
_____
_____
_____
_____

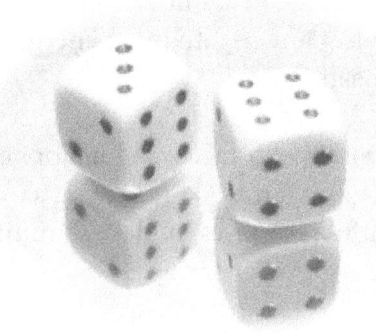

SECTION 8

Bringing it all Together

Bringing it all Together

Empowerment and accountability in entrepreneurship or your career are the drivers for sustainable success.

How do you define success in your career and work life?

_____

_____

_____

_____

Has it changed definitively in the course of reading this blueprint for success, or are you still refining your conception of a winning formula?

_____

_____

_____

_____

Profits and promotions can be objectives as well, but they should never be your primary focus. Money and status can be motivating to a point, but they will not bring you the drive and staying power of a goal that is intimately connected with who you are and what you truly value.

What Is Your Calling?

Success at its most fulfilling involves an alignment with a calling that defines one's professional life, but also enhances your personal life and fulfillment as a human being. The precise definition of success will, of course, differ in terms of tastes and personal preferences.

Refine your earlier definition of success from page 3.

_____

_____

_____

_____

There are many pathways up the mountain, and the road to success can take different forms. There is no one formula or roadmap that will be a fit for everyone. Use the diagram below to trace your pathway of success.

Bringing it all Together

How do the following qualities help you to commit to your goal?

1. Willingness to seek the required knowledge and education:

___

2. Ability to leverage existing resources:

___

3. Ability to remain transparent and self-aware:

___

4. Managing adversity and risk mitigation:

_____
_____
_____
_____

5. A healthy measure of patience:

_____
_____
_____
_____

Cultivating Leadership for A Winning Mindset

Again, a defining characteristic of a successful career includes the development of leadership qualities. While the ability to lead may manifest as rising to higher levels of management or more prominent roles in your business career, it can also take the form of your emergence as a thought leader in your field.

The qualities of effective leadership often emerge naturally as experience levels in your field continue to grow. However, the characteristics of effective leadership can also be cultivated

Bringing it all Together

through deliberate intention, focus and action. The desire to be a leader can move you along the path of self-development, but it is through experiences that the qualities of leadership are cultivated in an authentic way.

List some of your natural leadership qualities below:

_____

_____

_____

_____

_____

_____

This book was created to assist you in cultivating the empowerment and motivation to rise to greater levels of success and achievement than ever before. The value of self-empowerment, leadership ability, and seeking motivational resources that assist in enhanced personal development can be instrumental in helping you grow personally and attain new levels of success.

Essential Components of Success

All new achievements begin with the desire for success and new levels of accomplishment. Perhaps you've already been successful with setting and achieving goals but are aspiring to new heights. The fact that you've sought out this book says you're truly ambitious and wish to take your entrepreneurial endeavors or career to the next level.

"There is a mindset that defines and creates success, and it is foundational to any and all goals you set. Instead of being a mystical, elusive prize, success can be achieved by using straightforward, effective tools and concepts."

As we discussed throughout this text, the components of a winning strategy and sustainable success include the following basic phases and steps:

1. Prospect: The first phase of sustainable success involves prospecting for what's possible.

Bringing it all Together

2. Plan: Effective planning and preparation helps to set the stage for success and create a blueprint for the steps required to achieve your goal.

3. Execute: The Execution Phase is the time for bringing your vision to life. The time frame for this phase of goal achievement is the most variable.

Within each of these three phases, there are 10 components of success as follows:

- Commitment and Faithfulness
- Education
- Self-Sufficiency
- Transparency
- Self-Awareness
- Leverage
- Patience
- Infrastructure
- Adversity
- Risk Mitigation

As you learned, these components are not defined or applied the same within each phase. Understanding, successful application and mastery of these 10 components within the phases of Prospecting, Planning and Execution provides both knowledge of self and a template for sustainable success for any business or career goal.

"True success is available to everyone who has a desire to use their own talents and aptitudes to contribute in the world and enhance the lives of others."

Passion, the Driving Force of Success

We began this journey of exploring the recipe for a winning mindset with passion, and we will end with it. True passion can be hard to define and impossible to manufacture artificially, but it is undeniable when it is there. When it is allowed to flow freely, there is little that can stop it. Truly inspired passion comes from a place that transcends outer circumstances. It is a force that allows you to overcome challenges and obstacles and align with the creative forces of life itself.

When you pursue a goal from a place of true passion, nothing can stop you. The goal transcends career and personal objectives to become a true calling.

Bringing it all Together

As you consider the Prospect Phase for your next career objective, look inside yourself to see where your own true passions lie.

What inspires you each and every day?

_____
_____
_____
_____

What would you do even if you did not receive a paycheck?

_____
_____
_____
_____

What is it that you can offer that few if anyone else on Earth can?

_____
_____
_____
_____

The answers to these questions can point you in the direction of your true calling and goals that are an ideal fit for you to pursue. Choose wisely! Don't squander your time and life energy on goals that aren't deserving of your efforts. You will find them difficult to achieve, and you will not feel uplifted and inspired as you pursue them.

Instead, gravitate toward the goals and projects that make you feel truly alive and excited to be working on them. You will naturally connect with the partners, employees, and vendors to help make these goals a reality. Resources and related ideas will seem to "magically" flow into your life, and the pieces are far more likely to come together organically.

You are to be commended for taking this educational journey and seeing it through! Hopefully you have gained deeper insights into yourself as well as the ideal ways to approach new goals, career moves and projects. Apply the principles outlined here to each idea or objective and prepare to see how the benefits of going to the next level will enliven your spirit and enhance your life.

About Dr. Joseph D. Reid, CPA

Dr. Joseph D. Reid is a Certified Public Accountant (CPA) and a Chartered Global Management Accountant (CGMA). He is a professional member of the National Association of Black Accountants, the American Institute of Certified Public Accountants, the American Accounting Association and other industry associations. He received the Doctoral Student Teaching Award in 2011 and the KPMG Doctoral Consortium Fellowship in 2012. He has also received the 2015 40 under 40 Alumni Recognition Award from Winston-Salem State University.

Dr. Joseph Reid is also a serial entrepreneur, personal development and empowerment specialist, investor, business strategist and brand. He is a proponent of the values of empowerment, sustainable success, accountability and tapping into economic collectivism in entrepreneurship and personal goal achievement.

Dr. Reid is particularly experienced in the accounting space. He is highly experienced in all aspects of accounting, providing guidance to both individuals and business clients. He is a professor at North Carolina A&T State University, instructing the next generation of Auditing and Accounting professionals.

Dr. Reid provides value to his clients and audience through education and enlightenment, which leads to an expansion of perspective and an understanding of personal capacity through personal development and self-discovery. He is passionate about financial literacy, economic empowerment and educating others on how to leverage their assets to help create legacy and positive change. Dr. Reid took a non-traditional route in life and overcame both personal and financial obstacles to achieve significant success in both his academic life and professional achievements.

While he had no mentors to encourage him to go to college, he eventually sought a degree and was able to complete a four-year program in just two years. Dr. Reid earned his Bachelor of Accounting from Winston Salem State University. Three years later, he became a Certified Public Accountant while also continuing his educational path and earning his PhD in Accounting from the University of Memphis.

Dr. Reid runs the full-service Accounting Firm, Joseph Reid, CPA, PLLC, while also enjoying his role as an Assistant Professor at North Carolina Agricultural and Technical State University for over five years. He shares innovative curriculum with both MBA and undergraduate students in classes that include: Managerial Accounting, Financial Accounting, Not-for-Profit and Governmental Accounting, Auditing Principles and Seminar in Financial Concepts.

Dr. Reid also launched Mentors L.E.A.D. Inc during this time. Mentors L.E.A.D. is a nonprofit corporation that facilitates assisting students through connecting them with structured training that emphasizes the value of developing key life skills through personal development and leadership training. He has been published numerous times in a range of publications and has also been invited to speak at industry conferences across the United States and Europe. These events have included the Academic Business Research Institute, the Financial Reporting and Business Communication Conference and the European Annual Accounting Conference.

Dr. Reid's presentations cover fair value measurements, financial reporting quality, strategic alliances and firm performance in emerging markets and the relationship between information processing and student success. He has also delivered inspirational speeches to university and high school students, youth empowerment programs and faith based groups around the United States.

Dr. Reid has a personal goal of empowering as many people as he can to connect with direction and clarity related to their goals as well as effectively executing and achieving them. He believes cultivating a success mindset along with key tools for sustainable success are the formula for winning in all areas of life.

www.ingramcontent.com/pod-product-compliance
Lightning Source LLC
Chambersburg PA
CBHW052110070526
44584CB00017B/2418